Military Aircraft Library
Future Fighters

Military Aircraft Library
Future Fighters

DR. DAVID BAKER

Rourke Enterprises, Inc.
Vero Beach, FL 32964

Library of Congress Cataloging-in-Publication Data

Baker, David, 1944-
  Future fighters/by David Baker.

  p. cm. — (The Military aircraft series)
  Includes index.
  Summary: Describes the categories, functions, and individual types of military fighter planes of the past, present, and future.
  ISBN 0-86592-535-6
  1. Fighter planes — Design and construction — Juvenile literature [1. Fighter planes. 2. Airplanes, Military.]
I: Title. II. Series: Baker, David, 1944-   Military aircraft Library.
UG1242.F5B35   1989   88-33688
623.74'64 — dc19   CIP
                                        AC

CONTENTS

What Fighters Do

Fighter planes are among the most thrilling aircraft flying today. They are fast, maneuverable, powerful, and noisy. They are exciting to fly, and a flight in one beats a roller-coaster ride at the amusement park any day. Yet they are designed for a very specific set of duties, and they exist only to fight other planes in the sky or to attack enemy installations. Today, fighter planes can be divided into three different categories. Each category has a particular set of functions, and fighters are designed to carry out those functions efficiently, reliably, and at the least cost.

The division between the three categories of fighter planes can sometimes be difficult to see. The first category includes all the many different types designed to intercept *enemy threats*. A threat is said to be anything that comes to attack. It can be a bomber, an attack plane trying to bomb installations near the battlefield, another fighter, or a *guided missile* sent by the enemy to shoot something down.

This category is divided and named according to function. Some are called *interceptors*, because they go out to intercept enemy threats in the air. Others are called *air superiority fighters*, because they try to

Large fighters like this F-111 have been adapted as ground attack planes.

A swarm of F-16s fly in formation, on the lookout for enemy intruders.

Although light and agile, the F-16 can pack a powerful punch.

prevent the enemy from becoming superior in the air. Within these types, there are further sub-divisions. For instance, an *all-weather fighter* is one that is designed to fly in bad weather conditions, day or night. It must be capable of finding the enemy under any condition and of successfully using weapons against him.

Despite the wide variety of functions for this category, they all attempt to achieve the same thing:

control of the air space above a battlefield. This they do by finding and destroying the enemy opposition, a process called *counter-air*. Counter-air is the most popularly imagined role of the fighter plane and is one of the more important jobs for combat planes.

8

Dropping bombs is only one of several roles for which the F-16 is designed.

An enemy who controls the air above a battlefield can use its own *attack planes* to bomb ground forces, blow up bridges, and destroy tanks and artillery without challenge.

The second fighter plane category has developed from the belief that the best form of defense is offense. This does not mean that the best way to stop a war from starting is to destroy another country's armed forces so they could never be used against you. It does mean responding to an unprovoked attack by striking back very hard, deep behind the front line, to prevent the enemy from continuing the fight.

Strike fighters capable of hitting the enemy far inside his territory, day or night and in all kinds of weather, are seeking to destroy his reserves. This category is called *interdiction*, although some people refer to it as penetration strike or simply strike. Fighters that carry out this role are not bombers, because they are expected to fight their way in and possibly fight their way out of enemy-held airspace. When they have dropped their bomb loads or launched their long-range guided missiles, they must expect to have a rough ride home and to have punch left to knock out the enemy counter-air planes.

The third category, called *close air support*, aids troops on the ground and attacks enemy positions in and on the battlefield. Some people think these planes should be put into a completely separate group; they argue that they are not fighters at all but attack planes. This may be true, but they are included here because they are built to fight enemy planes as part of their range of duties.

The air force and the army both recognized that in a conflict they would be fighting the same enemy in the same area and that doing the job together was better than doing it individually. They developed the *airland battle* concept in which ground and air units work together, one supporting the other. Close air support will be a very important function for future fighters.

The navy has a similar but slightly different job for its fighters, which fly and fight from the floating decks of aircraft carriers. Two categories of fighters are in use by the navy. One, called air superiority, defends the carrier and its accompanying ships from attack by going out to meet and stop the enemy before he gets through. These planes have long-range, powerful *radars* and accurate guided missiles.

The second category belongs to the *multi-role fighter*. Planes that do this job for the navy operate over less distance to protect the carriers close in. They serve also as fighters in the counter-air role over land or beach operations. They also operate as ground attack planes, carrying bombs and rockets in an airland role for the navy and the marine corps. In all of these categories, the planes built to fly the missions are designed to outfight the threat.

In the heavyweight fighter class, the F-15 Eagle has been adapted to the ground attack role.

Northrop developed this F-20 fighter from a training plane, but it failed to attract customers.

The modern fighter is a gun platform with strong pylons for bombs, rockets, and missiles.

Threats

The nature of the air threat has changed significantly over time. In the early days of military aviation, fighters were built to do one of two jobs: find other fighters and shoot them down, or attack other enemy planes taking pictures or dropping bombs. The threat to the fighter was the enemy fighter flying against it, the gunners in the slow spy planes, and the bombers trying to defend themselves.

Heat-seeking missiles home in on the hot exhaust of a fighter's jet engine, a powerful beacon to infra-red weapons.

Powerful radar is the key to successful detection and identification of aircraft that fighter planes may be called upon to attack.

All modern fighters carry several different kinds of air-to-air missiles capable of attacking targets in the sky from a distance of a few miles to several tens of miles.

13

During World War Two (1939-45), radar brought an added dimension to the threat. Radar works by detecting reflected radio signals bounced off the surface of a plane in the sky. Even if the plane is too far away to see with the naked eye, radar will pick it up and tell of its presence. At first, radar was only a rough guide to what was coming and in which direction it was flying. Radar transmitters were located on the ground and used to send information to the pilots. Then, shortly after the war, fighter planes began to carry radar.

To lead heat-seeking missiles away from its jet engine, an F-16 releases hot flares as a decoy.

Not only could enemy planes be detected before they could be seen, individual fighter planes could now go hunting for the enemy without complex instructions from the ground. Radar helped speed

A fighter pilot checks the attachment pylon for one of his powerful Sidewinder missiles, capable of destroying an aircraft at a range of about ten miles.

Some heavy fighters double as ground attack planes, carrying guided weapons like this early Paveway missile.

up the interception and made fighters more vulnerable to attack. But the attack itself was speeded up when the jet engine was developed. Instead of flying propeller-driven planes no faster than 400 MPH, jet engines now boosted fighters to speeds greater than 1,000 MPH.

During the 1950s, another new dimension was added to the threat. *Heat-seeking missiles*, capable of going after the hot exhaust of jet engines, were developed. No longer did the pilot have to press home his attack by getting close enough to gun down the opposition. All he had to do was get within range, position the aircraft for attack, and release the missile.

In practice the heat-seekers were not nearly as good as they sounded. Planes could twist and turn more quickly than the charging missile, moving out of its way as it sped past. Planes could even throw out *flares* brighter than the exhaust plume to send the missile off to a false target. Then came radar-guided missiles; in these, a radio beam locked onto the target as the missile followed the beam down to the enemy plane or ground target.

Radar guidance was a more serious threat. In response, scientists and engineers developed *jammers* to upset the enemy radar and give it false messages. These worked with some effect but were soon countered with radar that could transmit a signal from the missile or launch plane to jam the jammer. This in turn gave rise to a range of new devices for what are now called *countermeasures* — measures taken to counter the electronic devices operated by the enemy. Today scientists and engineers are working feverishly to develop *counter-countermeasures*!

All this new technology, which took planes from 450 MPH in 1945 to 1,200 MPH just 10 years later, had its effect on the way people thought airplanes would be used in a future war. In 1945, bombers were believed to be the means by which an enemy would be subdued. Atomic weapons had been invented and were capable of destroying entire cities. High-flying bombers, heavily defended with guns and cannons, would roam at will over the enemy to drop their lethal loads.

The missile developments of the mid-1950s

provided an opportunity to improve anti-aircraft defenses greatly. The Soviets poured large sums of money into anti-aircraft missile defense and surrounded their country with a large number of powerful surface-to-air missiles *(SAMs)*. They were linked with radar to give warning of approaching planes and guaranteed that no bomber would survive for long. It was soon no longer possible to think of flying high and fast to targets deep inside enemy territory.

Instead of building fighters to go up high to get the high-flying bombers, fighters for counter-air or air-superiority duties were designed to keep close to the ground. Using the hills and valleys to mask radar,

which travels in straight lines, planes could sneak in under the radar screen and fight off attack planes and low-flying strike missions. This activity inspired the very latest threat to the fighter, the *look-down/shoot-down radar*.

For years, radar was not capable of looking down from a few thousand feet onto quickly moving targets far below. After much work, scientists finally found a solution to this problem. Now, instead of being threatened by ground radar looking up, fighters today are challenged by look-down/shoot-down radar and radar-guided missiles from enemy planes just above them in the air. In today's air war, there is no longer any place to hide.

Ground crew install a Sparrow missile on an F-15. The missile has a range of up to thirty miles.

Do We Need Fighters?

"The missile is never going to replace the man. Machines are not really very bright. Missiles will always have limitations compared to manned craft." So spoke General Curtis Le May, Chief of Staff of the United States Air Force in August 1961. Although he was right, many people thought otherwise and tried to prove that conflict was now a matter of "push-button" warfare. Push a button to launch a missile, push a button to fire a rocket, push a button to blow up a city.

The most serious decision about the continuing need for manned fighters in the missile age was made by Great Britain. That country stood alone in 1940 when all Europe had been invaded by Nazi Germany. Only Britain, isolated from mainland Europe, successfully resisted German attack. When German bombers and escorting fighters came to bomb towns and cities, the Royal Air Force sent Spitfire and Hurricane fighters to maintain control of the air.

The British did maintain control of the air over their country, and the Germans canceled plans to

By 1940, single-wing eight-gun fighters were capable of almost 400 MPH.

Early fighters were little more than wood, canvas, and wire, with one or two guns and a top speed of around 200 MPH.

Today the modern fighter is the first line of defense against intruding bombers and enemy strike planes; this powerful machine is capable of speeds greater than 1500 MPH.

Sometimes fighters are modified to do other duties; this F-111 has been converted into an electronic jamming plane and re-designated EF-111A.

invade. Without control of British airspace for parachute troops and beach landings on the coast, they could not go ahead. The Spitfire and Hurricane fighters saved the country and proved the importance of *air superiority*. Yet in 1957, the British government decided that in the future missiles would replace fighters.

The Royal Air Force was not allowed to place contracts with industry for British fighter planes. Instead, the British spent the next 30 years buying fighters from the United States or developing planes with European countries. The lesson to be learned is this: it is unwise to make such dramatic decisions without real evidence. Missiles have transformed aerial warfare, but they have not replaced the need for men to work the machines.

Modern fighters manned by well-trained pilots will be needed as far into the future as we can sensibly predict. Future fighters must be prepared to take on more threats than ever before, and technology will be stretched to the limit to match the fighter to those threats. To cut costs, several European countries are cooperating with each other to develop a new super fighter. Not only will they use it in their own air forces, but they can also sell it to other countries. Fighters make money as exports. In 1987, the sales from two U.S. fighter projects brought nearly $2 billion into the country. The same was true in 1988. America's vast aerospace industry is working around the clock to develop future fighters, both to combat the air threats of the next century and to bring export sales to the country.

The modern fighter is so expensive that sometimes several countries cooperate to build one they can all buy. The Europeans have worked together to produce this Tornado fighter and ground attack plane.

21

Adapted Fighters

Because new planes are expensive to produce, it only makes sense to make the best use of those around. Fighter planes need the latest technology in electronics and radar systems, but the basic design will usually suffice for a long time. The United States is coming to the point where an entire generation of fighter planes will need replacing. The newest operational combat planes were designed between 10 and 20 years ago. Within the next 5 to 10 years, they will have to be replaced.

To ease the air force and the navy into a new era of very different fighter technology, industry is adapting existing planes for new threats until the fresh designs appear. Adapted fighters are nothing new. When a good airframe is designed, it usually lasts for 20 or 30 years in a variety of different roles. The McDonnell Douglas F-4 Phantom is a classic example of this. Designed in the early 1950s as a carrier-based fighter and attack plane, it was bought

One of the most versatile aircraft with fighter forces today is the F-4 Phantom, still in widespread operational use.

Adapted from a conventional fighter plane design, the EF-111A provides a protective screen for friendly fighters by jamming enemy radars that may be used to detect their approach.

Some people believe the best fighter plane is a single-seat, lightweight aircraft with excellent maneuverability.

Some people prefer heavyweight fighters carrying two crew members, one to fly the plane, and the other to operate the radar and fire the weapons.

by the air force and then the marine corps. The Phantom served with many air forces around the world and is still in front-line service.

Adaptations of the basic airframe — adding better engines, improved electronics, or modern weapons — are common. There is, however, another form of adapted plane, the one that starts life in one role and ends up in a different one. The classic example here is the tiny Northrop T-38. Designed in the mid-1950s as a lightweight fighter, it was never produced as that

because the requirements of the air force changed and the plane no longer fit in.

Then it was submitted to the air force as a training plane for air force pilots. It was an instant success, and Northrop built more than 1,200 T-38 Talon trainers. Later the basic plane was modified by its manufacturer and considerably improved. It became the F-5 fighter, and more than 2,600 were sold to 31 countries. Large numbers are still in service, and Northrop even tried to develop it

Designed in the mid-1950s as a lightweight fighter, the F-5 has achieved fame as the T-38 trainer seen here.

The T-38 has been used to train candidate fighter pilots from many air forces around the world.

One of the most popular lightweight fighters in the world today, the F-16 has been sold to many friendly nations around the world and is used for a variety of duties.

further still into a more formidable warplane. That attempt was unsuccessful, but the basic design had already had an astonishing record as a trainer and light fighter.

Today, several planes with the air force and the navy are getting an extended lease on life by re-design and adaptation. The need for completely new fighters has increased faster than they can be put together. It is essential that the new technology for next century's powerful warplanes is first tested on proven planes. Technology for future fighters is currently being tested on today's planes.

The F-16 is one of the most up-to-date fighters available today, yet it, too, can be improved. Engineers are working hard to test new techniques for increasing the F-16's maneuverability and agility in the air. It is already one of the most agile fighters around. It can out-turn almost every other plane and has gained the envy of fighter pilots in foreign air forces around the world. It is a very powerful air

Heavy fighter planes like this F-111 may not be very good at the twists and turns of high-performance combat, but they do carry an enormous warload of rockets and bombs.

superiority plane and represents a category that the U.S. wants to improve even more.

Consider this. When you go for a ride on a roller coaster, you may pull twice your own weight in the twists and turns as the car follows the curves of the track. This is called 2g, which means you experience twice the force of gravity. Astronauts riding the space shuttle into orbit experience a force of 3g for several minutes as they rocket beyond the atmosphere.

Fighter pilots in planes like the F-16 can experience 9g or 10g in violent twists and turns in the air. This is close to the limit the human body can stand, yet agility gives the fighter a chance to survive because quick twists and turns in the air are the only way to escape charging missiles or other planes. It is also close to the structural limits of the airplane, and new materials must be found that can resist these stresses.

General Dynamics, makers of the F-16, are improving the fighter in what they call the Agile

Built by General Dynamics, the highly successful F-16 is being continually developed and improved.

Falcon program. By changing the shape of the wing and the control surfaces that govern the plane's attitude in flight, they can give extra lift to the plane, which makes it more agile. Lift keeps a plane in the air, and the wings are designed to achieve just the right amount of lift for good flying characteristics.

Engineers, too, are struggling to improve the way air flows around the wing and the nose of the F-16. By studying the pattern of the air as it meets the plane in flight, they can make minor adjustments to the exact location of flaps and control surfaces on the front edge of the wing. These help develop a very precise map of the air currents under a wide range of flight conditions. It is work like this that lays the groundwork for fighters in the twenty-first century.

Wings of the Future

Conventional wings are usually straight or swept back towards the tail. Swept wings were developed in the 1940s and contributed greatly to the handling of fast jets. Soon most fighters carried swept wings. Now, with computers designed to control the balance of a plane in the air, engineers are redesigning the wing again. Instead of sweeping back, Grumman's X-29 has wings that sweep forward. Forward-swept wings bring many advantages to fast, agile planes and are a great promise for the future. Still they have a big drawback.

Forward-swept wings come under rigorous stresses and strains that threaten to break the wings off completely. Ordinary metals, like stainless steel

The shape of a fighter's wing dictates its performance and is an important part of providing a highly maneuverable and agile design for all flying conditions.

and titanium, are light but do not have the strength needed to resist the force of air as it tears at the wing. Researchers have looked into new materials, including super-strength plastics and materials made of many different substances. After many experiments, they have developed material strong enough to resist air forces yet light enough to be used on the aircraft.

The X-29 has been flying test missions since April 1985, and engineers have collected valuable

The F-16's conventional wing has been developed into a new shape to give the aircraft better performance under certain flying conditions.

European fighters like this French-built Rafale are using improved design techniques and lightweight materials in their construction.

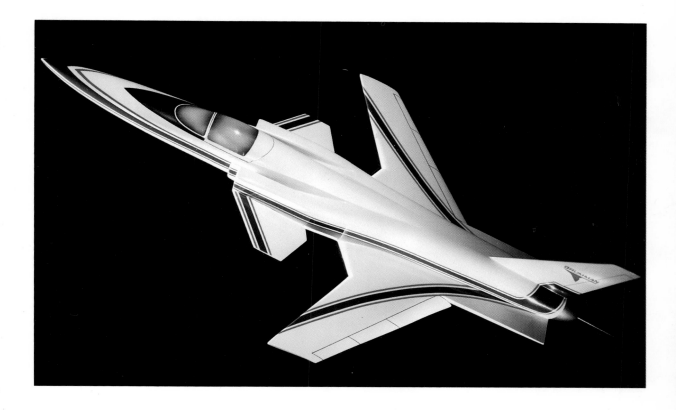

Grumman Aerospace built this exciting and revolutionary aircraft to test the idea that forward-swept wings would significantly improve performance in future fighter planes.

information about the advantages of a forward-swept wing design. The X-29 was not built to be a fighter but to help engineers study revolutionary design concepts for future applications. It is 48 feet, 1 inch in length and has a wing span of 27 feet, 2 inches. The wing is very thin — only 7 inches thick at the place where it is joined to the fuselage.

In preparation for the new generation of fighters, Rockwell International is building the X-31 under a cooperative agreement with the German firm of MBB (Messerschmitt-Boelkow-Blohm). This plane will have a conventional wing but is designed to study the problem of stall and how stall attitudes can be used to a pilot's advantage. This work will lead to a better and more maneuverable combat fighter in the future.

A plane stalls when it does not get the lift it needs to stay in the air. This usually happens because the plane has slowed down to a speed where it no longer generates lift from its wings and tail. Stall can occur if the nose of the plane is pulled up sharply or made to point at too high a pitch angle. Pilots always try to avoid stall. If it happens at a low altitude, the plane usually crashes because there is not enough air space to regain control.

In all the twists and turns of modern air combat, a plane can easily get into an attitude where it is pointing up at a high angle. In this condition, speed drops off, and the plane loses lift and drops like a stone. Planes that didn't stall in this situation would have a great advantage in combat. The fighter pilot could use high pitch-up angles to outwit and out-maneuver his opponents. In the X-31, Rockwell is developing such a plane.

Rockwell plans to build two X-31s. Each plane will have a length of 42 feet, 6 inches and a wing span

31

The forward-swept wing on the X-29 is built from special lightweight materials much stronger than steel and able to resist enormous aerodynamic forces on the plane in flight.

The wing of the X-29 is a single structure that carries right through the body of the plane and gives it great strength.

This experimental HiMAT was built and flown to test new wing and control surfaces, which engineers believed would make fighters more maneuverable in the air.

of 22 feet, 9 inches. Two vertical fins at the rear will be slanted outward to give the plane stability in unusual flying attitudes. Two horizontal finlets at the front will give added control of the plane's attitude in the air. The X-31 will be powered by a General Electric *turbofan engine*. Flight tests are expected to take place for several years in the early 1990s.

In combination with its special wing and control surfaces that provide extraordinary maneuverability, the X-31 will also have a swiveling engine exhaust nozzle. This will be used in tests to see if pilots can change the direction of exhaust and thereby alter the direction the plane is flying. If so, the snap maneuver would remove the plane from the missile sights of an enemy fighter.

In the heat of a fast-moving *dogfight*, the pilot's term for air-to-air combat, flick maneuvers and snap direction change may be the only way to escape. Survivability in the air depends very often on quick reaction and lightning reponse. If the plane can move as fast as a man can think, both may live to fight another day.

Super Cockpit

Fighter aces of the twenty-first century will have to counter swarms of heat-seeking bullets that change course in mid-air with tiny rocket motors, lasers, beam weapons, and more. Dodging high-speed missiles and lit by enemy radar, the manned combat plane will be a high technology office where a day's work is done at almost the speed of sound. No longer will it be enough for the man to blend in with the airplane as a single fighting system. He will have to be literally plugged in to the plane's complex and intelligent electronics.

To accomplish that, the air force is developing a helmet for the fighter pilot to wear that will provide him with better information than his own eyes and ears can. The helmet will literally cover his head,

Whatever the shape of the future fighter, its primary purpose will remain unchanged — to seize control of the skies and to dominate the air as long as national objectives require.

and like a rocket jockey from a *Star Wars* movie, he will get his flight information directly from the brain of the plane. The helmet will project a view of the world outside onto the inside of his faceplate. In this way, the pilot is not restricted to the limited view his eyes would get if he looked through the windscreen. He also gets computer graphics and images of what the heat-seeking sensors and the radar see.

For the pilot, it will be like flying through a

computerized video game, only he is part of the action on the screen. As the plane flies along it picks up information about the surrounding ground. It turns the murky view outside into a colorful graphics display on the inside of the helmet. Hills and valleys reveal the contours of the ground as grid lines in a math book, but folded to the actual shape of the land below. On the grid, symbols tell the pilot the locations of enemy radar sites and the route to fly to avoid these sites and other obstacles ahead.

Missile sites are pinpointed, coded letters identify the range of each enemy missile so the pilot knows how close to go, and approaching fighters are tracked as moving plane shapes. Information about those planes comes thick and fast, only the vital details flashing up on the graphic screen. The pilot is given a pre-planned course to an important ground target, and on his screen a ribbon of light threads a

Although fighter planes today are packed with complex electronic gadgets, pilots still have manual control of much of the aircraft and its systems.

Large fighter planes like the Tornado, which also doubles as a ground attack aircraft, have two cockpits. This is the pilot's seat.

The rear cockpit of a two-seat Tornado carries radar screens for important information that is displayed to the weapons systems officer.

path through the contours of hills and valleys to show him that course. He quickly checks that the pre-selected route is still the one he chooses to fly and switches on the three-dimensional attack box.

With this he sits as though in a stereo sound system. As the radar detects approaching fighter planes, perhaps from the rear, he hears a simulated howl of a jet engine behind his head. That gives him the cue to switch scenes. He puts the plane on autopilot, telling it to do whatever is necessary to out-maneuver enemy planes that suddenly appear from the front and switches displays to a rearward-looking view. He is now no longer looking in the direction of flight but backwards. Instead of seeing the contoured grid lines rushing toward him, they are speeding away as he stares back along his flight path.

Suddenly, racing to catch up, two enemy fighters are fast approaching, threading their way through the valleys, chasing him but gaining ground. He grips a small control stick on the arm rest of his seat and a light comes on in his helmet display. As he slowly moves the stick it draws the light down onto the area where the planes are chasing him. Small symbols of

Future cockpits will increasingly rely on electronic displays and computer screens to provide the pilot with complex information. Note the single control column with gun- and missile-firing buttons.

his weapons flash on to the screen. He must choose which to use. He selects a missile, moves the symbol on to the plane shape and presses the button. A voice tells him the weapons are armed, fired, and on track.

Not waiting to watch what happens, the pilot switches back to the forward view, and the graphics appear to show him how far the plane has traveled in the meantime. The simulated roar of the approaching planes gets louder and suddenly a wailing sound tells the pilot they now have him within range of their own missiles. What to do? He knows it will take about 30 seconds for his own missiles to reach their targets. Fired forward from the fuselage, they will turn completely around at high speed and race back to attack the fighters head on. He also knows it would take several seconds for the enemy fighters to fire off a missile.

Without switching displays he flicks another switch on the arm rest and a small square appears in the top left-hand corner of the main helmet screen. It

Six flat-panel color display screens give the pilot vital information about his or her tactical environment and continuously advise about which targets pose the greatest threat.

Television displays provide the future pilot with all the information he or she needs to seek out and destroy approaching enemy aircraft, at close range or at great distance.

shows him a condensed view of what is going on behind. He need not switch back to full rear-facing view, since he just wants to monitor what is going on behind. A second later there is the simulated sound of an explosion behind his head, followed an instant later by a second explosion. This is the computer telling him he has achieved a direct hit. Up comes a readout on the screen recording the event and informing the pilot what weapons he has left. On the tiny screen inset he sees the two plane shapes vanish and knows they will be no further threat.

The pilot's head is plugged into the plane's electronic sensors, but extra detail comes by plugging the pilot's brain into the computer. With wires attached to the pilot's head, responding to his thoughts and the movement of his eyes, the computer will obey unspoken orders. If the pilot stares down at one corner of the graphic image, the computer sees him doing that and provides more detail.

This may allow a data file to appear on the screen above the object that comes ever nearer in the graphics as he flies toward it. If he wants to change pages on the data file he asks the computer by speaking coded words. The information and data display computer hears his request and, again, obeys. When he gets nearer the target the plane is

Three-dimensional images displayed on the inside of this pilot's helmet provide all the electronic information the pilot needs to understand how best to carry out his or her mission.

Fighter planes of the future will have only a vague resemblance to modern combat planes, and engineers are working hard to give this type of aircraft amazing new capabilities.

placed on fully automatic control and programmed to avoid enemy fighters and control the weapons needed to shoot them down. The pilot, meanwhile, concentrates on selecting the weapons for the target and setting up the radar and laser guidance systems.

This scenario is just one idea of how the future super cockpit will give the pilot a new edge over less advanced designs. The air force expects that within ten years fighter pilots will have this kind of system, in one form or another. Advanced electronics and computers that plug into a human head to listen, talk, think, and respond will be the additional crew member that will accompany every single-seat fighter pilot in the next century.

This picture shows the view inside the helmet, with contour lines depicting the rise and fall of land masses. Yellow boxes represent enemy aircraft and ground radar, red represents enemy forces, and white posts the pilot's recommended flight path to the target.

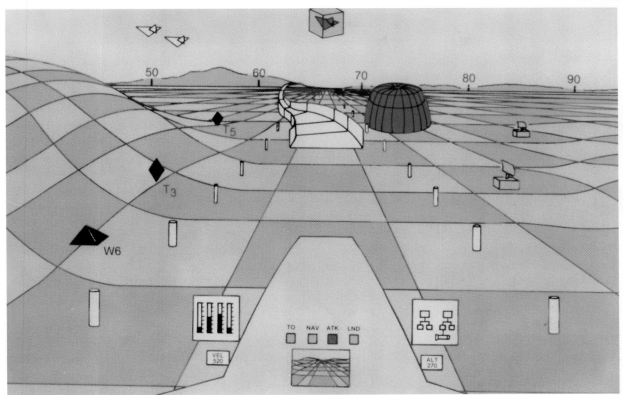

Super Plane

Wings that move forward and back in flight and engine air inlets on top of the fuselage may be a common sight on future fighters.

What will the future fighter look like? Some planes exist today that give a hint of that. In the United States, the work on the air force Advanced Tactical Fighter, or *ATF,* is under way. Two are being built, but only one will be ordered into production. A team headed by Lockheed will build the YF-22A and another team, headed by Northrop, will put together the YF-23A. They are being built to serve the air force and possibly the navy as well. The air force wants to replace its McDonnell Douglas F-15 Eagle all-weather air-superiority fighters. The navy wants to replace its F-14 Tomcat fleet-defense fighters.

The ATF will be highly maneuverable and have special characteristics that make it almost invisible on radar. That would be an enormous advantage, and the air force has been working secretly for many years on what it calls "stealth" technology. Radar

works by bouncing radio signals off the surface of an aircraft in flight. If the plane is designed so that most of the radio signals do not bounce back but are deflected away, those signals will not return to the antenna that sent them and the plane will be difficult to detect.

Certain materials can absorb radio waves, soaking them up like paper towels soak up water. If this material covers the outside of the plane, it will soak up many of the radio signals and further reduce the chances of detection. Moreover, complex counter-countermeasures, or electronic jammers, can hide the presence of the plane even more by disguising the source of the jammer. The radar operator on the ground or in the enemy fighter would think it was something else distorting the information on his screen.

This prototype of a future European fighter plane is put through its paces over the sea, where the new tactics and flying characteristics of these complex planes are first tested.

Lockheed has come up with this design for an Advanced Tactical Fighter, engineered for high reliability and low maintenance time.

Quick turns, agility, and high maneuverability are the three key elements of future fighters now being designed in many countries around the world.

Europe is also building a super fighter for the next century. It is called *EAP*, for Experimental Aircraft Program. Britain is flying this plane under an agreement with West Germany and Italy. EAP has many advanced features, such as a special wing for high maneuverability and an electronic flight control system that can balance the plane far better than any pilot ever could.

Britain is also involved in the *EFA*, or European Fighter Aircraft, program which also includes West Germany, Italy, and Spain. European countries are expected to buy 800 planes in the 1990s, following a first flight planned for 1992. This super fighter will have amazing maneuverability and agility and a combat radius of more than 300 miles from base. The plane will carry up to 5 tons of weapons on any

As part of a cooperative venture with West Germany, the United States is developing this Enhanced Fighter Maneuverability plane, which will be tested in the air during the early 1990s.

of up to 15 different pylons under the wings and the fuselage.

Future fighters will look a lot different than the planes of today. They will be complex, expensive, and highly sophisticated machines. In some ways, they will be robots with human operators instead of pilots. Nevertheless, the demand for flying skills and high levels of training will increase rather than decline. Combined with the firepower of modern weapons, the manned fighter of the twenty-first century will be a formidable combat plane.

GLOSSARY

Airland battle	Battlefield operations involving the close cooperation of ground and air units working together and supporting each other.
Air superiority	Control of friendly or enemy airspace.
Air superiority fighter	An aircraft built to gain control of the skies over friendly or unfriendly territory by attacking and destroying enemy aircraft in the air.
All-weather fighter	A fighter designed to fly in bad weather conditions, day or night, under extremely hazardous atmospheric conditions.
Advanced Tactical Fighter (ATF)	An airplane being developed by the United States Air Force to replace existing fighter planes.
Attack planes	Aircraft designed and built to attack ground targets.
Close air support	The use of aircraft to attack ground targets and enemy positions on the battlefield in support of friendly forces.
Counter-air	Gaining control of the air space above the battlefield by finding and destroying the enemy.
Countermeasures	Electronic devices designed to jam enemy radar or electronic equipment.
Counter-countermeasures	Electronic equipment designed to deceive countermeasures equipment operated by another aircraft or ground units.
Dogfight	The pilot's term for air-to-air combat between fighter planes.
Experimental Aircraft Program (EAP)	A European project designed to develop the technology needed for the next generation of fighter planes.
European Fighter Aircraft (EFA)	A cooperative program between West Germany, Italy, Spain, and Britain to develop a super-fighter for the next century.
Enemy threats	Any piece of land, sea, or air equipment designed to attack army, navy, or air force units in time of war.
Flares	Bright sources of heat similar to firecrackers. When ejected from an aircraft, flares attract heat-seeking missiles and throw them off course.
Guided missile	A missile that is guided all the way to its target rather than being pointed in a specific direction and left to fly of its own accord.
Heat-seeking missiles	Missiles with small infra-red devices designed to lock onto the hot exhaust of an aircraft engine.
Interceptors	Fighter planes designed to attack approaching enemy aircraft.
Interdiction	Action conducted by strike fighters; sometimes called penetration strike.
Jammers	Electronic signals sent out by an aircraft or by a ground device to jam the radio or radar equipment of an enemy aircraft or ground unit.

Look-down/ shoot-down radar	Radar units designed to look down at low-flying aircraft or helicopters and detect them against the background of the earth's surface.
Multi-role fighter	A fighter plane adapted to more than one different task, such as ground attack and air superiority.
Radar	**Ra**dio **D**etection **A**nd **R**anging. A system of detecting objects by bouncing radio signals off them.
Strike fighters	Fighters converted to a ground attack role and designed to fly day or night and in all kinds of weather; sometimes called interdiction.
Surface-to-Air Missiles (SAM)	Missiles launched from the ground to attack aircraft in the air between short and long range.
Turbofan engine	A jet engine with blades arranged in a circle like a fan to increase the amount of air delivered to the combustion chamber.

INDEX

Page references in *italics* indicate photographs or illustrations.